STRATHMORE HIGH SCHOOL
100 Brent Blvd.
Strathmore, AB   T1P 1V2
Tel. (403) 934-3135

UNDERSTANDING IMMIGRATION

A Multicultural World

Iris Teichmann

Smart Apple Media

First published in 2005 by Franklin Watts
96 Leonard Street, London EC2A 4XD

Franklin Watts Australia
Level 17/207 Kent Street
Sydney NSW 2000

Series editor: Rachel Cooke
Series design: Simon Borrough
Picture research: Diana Morris

Published in the United States by Smart Apple Media
2140 Howard Drive West, North Mankato, Minnesota
56003

Library of Congress Cataloging-in-Publication Data

Teichmann, Iris.
A multicultural world / by Iris Teichmann.
p. cm. — (Understanding immigration)
Includes index.
ISBN-13 : 978-1-58340-969-5
1. Multiculturalism—Juvenile literature. 2. Pluralism
(Social sciences)—Juvenile literature. 3. Emigration
and immigration—Juvenile literature. I. Title.

HM1271.T45 2006
305.8—dc22   2005051733

9 8 7 6 5 4 3 2 1

Acknowledgements: Alexander the Great's story,
p.10, Michael Bakaoukas, "Tribalism and Racism
among the Ancient Greeks," Anistoriton, Vol. 9, March
2005; China's story, p.11, Herbert A. Giles, "The
Civilization of China," Historical Text Archive 2003,
historicaltextarchive. com; The Wichí Indians' story,
p.12, Survival International, www.survival-
international.org; The Norwegian-Americans' story,
p.13, The Norwegian-American Historical Association,
Northfield, MN; Abigail Adams's story, p.14, Laurie
Carter Noble, *Abigail Adams*, Unitarian Universalist
Historical Society; Thomas Macaulay's story, p.15,
"Minute on Indian Education," humanitas.ucsb.edu;
Liang Qichao's story, p.17, "Selected Memoirs of
Travels in the New World," xroads.virginia.edu; A
Greek Australian's story, p.18, Alexandra Holvea,
"Current Trends of the Linguistic and Cultural Values
of the Greek Australian Community in South
Australia," International Education Journal, Vol. 4,
No. 4, 2004; Vince Reid's story, p.19,
www.bbc.co.uk/history; Malika's story, p.21, "The
Integration Paper: The Contributors," For Diversity
Against Discrimination, Journalist Award 2004
campaign, www.ja04.stop-discrimination.info; Zerife's
story, p.22, www.denmark.dk; Moris Farhi's story, p.23,
Exiled Ink!, No. 1, 2003; Hansa's story, p.24, *Hansa's
Indian Vegetarian Cookbook*, Hansa's Publications, 2000;
Tsoarnelo's story, p.25, www.rage.co.za; A typical
story, p.26, www.bangla.ca; Aïcha's story, p.27, Aïcha
Benaïssa, *Née en France*, 2000, Pocket; John A. Powell's
story, p.28, California News Reel, 2003,
www.pbs.org/race; Sylvia's story, p.29, The Legal Aid
Society Employment Law Center; Dyab Abou Jahjah's
story, p.32, "The Many Faces of Islam," *Time*,
01/08/05; Joanne's story, p.33, Joanne Richmond, *My
Heritage is Franco-American*, Unitarian University
History Society, www.uua.org; Pavi's story, p.34,
www.excelsis.cc/weblog/pavi/archives/cat_people.php;
Fadime's story, p.35, www.cnn.com, 02/05/2002, and
Aftonbladet, 02/04/2002; Vaira Vike-Freiberga's story,
p.36, United Nations High Commissioner for
Refugees; Jennifer's story, p.37, Jun-yung Ahn, *Korea
Daily News*, 05/12/03; Jette's story, p.38, Jette Englund
Smith, 1997, unbound.intrasun.tcnj.edu/archives/
government/old/american.html; Shane's story, p.39,
Aetna Smith, "Identity Squeeze: What Irks Mixed-Race
Americans in Daily Life," www.jru.columbia.edu;
Camilla's story, p.40, Camilla Pedersen, "The Search
for Normal," www.onvik.com.

Photographic credits: Vicky Alhadett/Lebrecht/
Alamy: p.23. Archivberlin Fotoagentur GmbH/Alamy:
p.33. Craig Aurness/Corbis: p.18. David Brauchli/
Sygma/Corbis: p.21. David Butow/Saba/Corbis: p.37.
Peter Casolino/Alamy: p.25. Jackie Chapman/
Photofusion: p.27. Coo-ee Picture Library: p.16.
Christopher Cormack/Impact Photos: p.32. Michael
Fresco/Rex Features: p.35. Sally Greenhill/Sally &
Richard Greenhill: p.41. Richard Greenhill/Sally &
Richard Greenhill: pp.9, 20, 24. Ute Klaphake/
Photofusion: front cover b, pp.2, 3, 4, 45, 46, 47. Erich
Lessing/Louvre, Paris/AKG Images: p.10bl. Gunter
Marx Photography/Corbis: p.22. Ulli Michel/Corbis:
p.28. Maggie Murray/Photofusion: p.26. Naglestock.
com/Alamy: p.11. Joanne O'Brien/Photofusion: pp.29,
31. John Palmer/Survival International: p.12.
Pinacoteca Capitolina, Palazzo Conservatori, Rome,
Italy/Giraudon/Bridgeman Art Library: p.10tr.
Popperfoto: p.19. Ulrike Preuss/Photofusion: front
cover t, pp.8, 34. J.B. Russell/Panos Pictures: p.40.
Rykoff Collection/Corbis: p.17. Christa Stadtler/
Photofusion/Alamy: p.36. David Turnley/Corbis: p.39.
Eileen Tweedy/Terry Engell Gallery/Art Archive: p.13.
Upperhall/Robert Harding: p.15. Deng Yai: p.30. Yale
Center for British Art, Paul Mellon Collection,
USA/Bridgeman Art Library: p.14. Michael S.
Yamashita/Corbis: p.38.

Contents

What is multiculturalism?

A crowd enjoys an open-air concert. Today's societies are made up of an increasingly diverse mix of people.

What is culture?

Most people use the word "culture" to describe activities in the worlds of music, art, literature, and film. But culture is much more than that. It is the way of life that is passed on from one generation to another. It includes the language people learn as they grow up and the customs, ideas, values, and types of behavior taught by families. Culture changes as people learn about the ideas and values of others.

Becoming multicultural

Today, many people live alongside others from very different cultures—societies have become multicultural ones. A multicultural society is one in which people from different cultures live together. Cultural diversity tends to be promoted and celebrated in these societies, but there are still considerable differences in the way people from different racial and cultural backgrounds are treated, especially if they are in a minority.

Old news

The modern multicultural world has developed as a result of immigration patterns in the 19th and 20th centuries. Starting in the 1800s, an unprecedented number of people moved from eastern and central Europe—and later from all over the world—to seek a better life, freedom, and security in the West (North America, Australasia, and western Europe). But there is nothing new about multiculturalism itself. Throughout history, civilizations have influenced other civilizations through conquest, migration, and trade.

Culture clash

History shows that where people with different physical appearances, behavior, and beliefs live together, there is almost always tension. At a basic human level, tension arises because people are fearful or suspicious of those from other cultures and races, and can find it difficult to tolerate them or consider them equal. Tensions, however, can hide the positive aspects of different people living together. From the way people eat and shop to their beliefs and art, multicultural societies enrich lives.

Many Western cities are multicultural places, where people from different cultures tolerate and learn from each other.

AS A MATTER OF FACT

Race: A group of people with common physical characteristics. The Caucasian race, for example, refers to people of white skin color of European, Middle Eastern, and North African descent.

Ethnic group: Each race has many different ethnic groups. In turn, each ethnic group has its own culture, ancestry, and homeland, and often language, too.

Ethnic minority: An ethnic group that forms only one part of a larger group in society. For example,

black people form an ethnic minority in the United States and Britain, while white people are an ethnic minority in South Africa and the Middle East.

Nation: A community of people—who may belong to different ethnic groups—that shares a common territory and often, although not always, has its own government. It may also share a common culture. For example, people of many different backgrounds celebrate Thanksgiving Day in the U.S.

Cultural encounters in the past

Cultural exchange

Different cultures have been influencing one another for thousands of years. Ancient Greeks colonized Italy and parts of Asia Minor (modern-day Turkey), spreading their culture while at the same time encouraging trade. From their home in Italy, Romans set up colonies as far away as Britain. Romans encouraged their subjects to adopt Roman culture. If people did not give up their own customs and beliefs, they remained foreigners in society, but they were still tolerated.

Barbarians and Greeks

Like the Romans, the ancient Greeks had a notion of difference based more on culture than physical appearance. They viewed anyone who did not speak their language as a "barbarian." But if foreigners did learn the language and adopted Greek customs, they were not only able to integrate better but also able to gain status in the same way as any other Greek.

This Greek vase, from about 480 B.C., depicts two market traders. Trade is an ancient way for cultures to come into contact with each other.

ALEXANDER THE GREAT'S STORY: EARLY MULTICULTURALISM

Alexander the Great (356–323 B.C.) expanded the empire of the ancient Greeks and spread Greek civilization and culture. In 326 B.C., he reached India, where he made this appeal:

"I do not separate people as many narrow-minded others do into Greeks and Barbarians. I'm not interested in the origin of race of citizens. I only distinguish them on the basis of their virtue. For me, each good foreigner is a Greek, and each bad Greek is a barbarian.... For my part, I consider all, whether they be white or black, equal, and I would like you to be not only the subjects of my commonwealth, but also participants and partners."

Absorbing other cultures

Between 206 B.C. and A.D. 220, China's emperors, from the largest ethnic group, the Han, also unified different groups of people into one dominant culture. As a result, people from outside the Chinese empire were viewed with suspicion and even considered a threat to its culture. Both during the Han dynasty and many times after, China was influenced by influxes of people from outside its borders, but this fearful attitude toward outsiders continued up to the modern age.

CHINA'S STORY: GETTING USED TO THE "FOREIGN DEVILS"

Writing in the early 20th century, English scholar of Chinese language and culture Herbert A. Giles described the Chinese attitude to foreigners:

"The Chinaman may love you, but you are a devil all the same. It is most natural that he should think so. For generation upon generation, China was almost completely isolated from the rest of the world. The people of her vast empire grew up under influences unchanged by contact with other peoples. Their ideals became stereotyped from want of other ideals to compare with, and possibly modify, their own.... Then the foreign devil [Europeans] burst upon the scene.... Small wonder that little children are terrified at these strange beings and rush shrieking into their cottages as the foreigner passes by."

The Great Wall of China runs for about 4,150 miles (6,700 km) across northern China. It was completed in the third century B.C. to protect the country from invaders.

11

A modern-day Wichí Indian.

THE WICHÍ INDIANS' STORY: LOSING LAND AND LIVELIHOOD

In the 17th century, European colonists invaded the land of the Wichí Indians in Argentina. A modern-day Wichí tells what happened to his ancestors:

"We call the colonists *ahatai,* which is like our words for 'spirit of the dead' (*ahat*) and for 'the devil' (*ahataj*). The ahatai...used deceit and violence in order to take [our land] from us. At first, they deceived our leaders by telling them that they wanted to borrow some grasslands for just a few months in order to graze their cattle. Our ancestors were not mean about land, and the leaders allowed the new arrivals to use it for a short while in exchange for some tobacco, beef, and metal tools. But, by the end of a year, the ahatai had built houses and corrals; they had moved all their livestock onto the land, including horses, goats, sheep, and pigs, and they had no intention of leaving."

New World conquerors

From the 16th century onward, European powers built empires by conquering territory overseas and exploiting the land and resources of indigenous peoples. The Europeans' initial contact with native tribes was often violent, but both sides tried to benefit from each other. The colonists needed to communicate with tribal leaders to acquire food and learn about the land and its resources. The tribal leaders, in turn, were often happy to obtain goods from the Europeans, which could raise their status and power.

Exploitation

For the most part, the colonizing Europeans viewed the natives they encountered as people without culture or true religion, referring to them as "savages." The colonists saw themselves as a superior culture, and their missionaries tried to convert the natives to Christianity. As different European powers competed for their slice of colonies overseas, indigenous peoples increasingly suffered. Their land was taken away, they were often forced to work in appalling conditions, and their access to food and other resources could be severely restricted.

To settle or not

For the most part, European colonists were interested in exploiting resources and less interested in setting up permanent settlements. In contrast, North America was regarded as a virtual wilderness that was ideal for settlement and development. The first Europeans to arrive there were the British, but other settlers soon followed. The majority were motivated to start a new life and to shape a new identity. Others, however, found life hard and tried to maintain their own cultural identity.

THE NORWEGIAN-AMERICANS' STORY: A DIFFICULT START

In 1847, Norwegian Consul-General Adam Løvenskjold visited Wisconsin, where about 7,500 Norwegians lived. Many of the settlers he visited complained about their new life in America. Løvenskjold wrote that the settlers were living **"to a large extent in sod huts almost underground, with only the roofs projecting above the surface."**

Many had not yet learned English and knew little about American life or its political institutions. He added that other Americans called the settlers "Norwegian Indians," comparing them to the Native American Indians whom they looked down on.

Future North American settlers prepare for their long journey from Europe in the early 1600s. Many settlers escaped religious persecution in Europe to build new communities overseas.

An English lord, hunting with his black servant, in a painting from about 1765. Many more black people worked for white masters in the Caribbean and the Americas than in Europe.

The slave trade

Colonization brought with it the enslavement of African people to work on plantations in the European colonies. When Africans were first shipped to North America, they worked alongside poor European laborers under the same harsh conditions. But toward the end of the 17th century, colonial laws began to separate the African slaves from the European laborers.

Distinguishing black from white

Slavery became increasingly important for the European economies, and African slaves began to be referred to as "Negroes." In Europe and the Americas, a clear distinction arose between whites, who had privileges, rights, and power, and blacks, who had none. To justify their denial of equality and rights to black people, white Europeans and Americans developed theories that blacks were inferior to whites. In the late 1700s, it was up to individuals to speak out for black people.

ABIGAIL ADAMS'S STORY: SPEAKING OUT

Abigail Adams (1744–1818) was the wife of the second U.S. president, John Adams. When a black servant boy, the son of a freed slave, came to her asking to learn to write, she enrolled him in a local school. In response to criticisms of her action, she wrote:

"[The boy is] a freeman as much as any of the young men, and merely because his face is black, is he to be denied instruction? How is he to be qualified to procure a livelihood? I have not thought it any disgrace to myself to take him into my parlor and teach him both to read and write."

THOMAS MACAULAY'S STORY: CULTURAL SUPERIORITY

In 1843, the British government sent politician and writer Thomas Macaulay to India to decide on the language for a national education system. Some argued that Indian people should be taught in Sanskrit or Arabic, but Macaulay insisted on English, at least for the most able Indians who would work for the British government in India.

"The dialects commonly spoken among the natives of this part of India contain neither literary nor scientific information and are, moreover, so poor and rude that, until they are enriched from some other quarter, it will not be easy to translate any valuable work into them.... We must at present do our best for a class who may be interpreters between us and the millions whom we govern; a class of persons, Indian in blood and color, but English in taste, in opinions, in morals, and in intellect."

Modern-day Calcutta, India's largest city. English remains one of the most widely used languages in India—a remnant of the time when Britain ruled the country.

A difficult legacy

Some people argue that the discrimination against black people during the slave trade, when it was the norm for white people to have power and rights over black people, still influences Western attitudes toward race. Others argue that these attitudes predate the slave trade, because they were clearly held by the European conquerors of South America, southern Asia (including India), and Africa. Many European colonists wrote that native tribes had "lax morals" and that they were uncultured.

15

Into the melting pot

In the 19th and early 20th centuries, millions of people from southern and eastern Europe attempted to put poverty and persecution behind them, moving to the U.S., Canada, Australia, and South America. The arrival of so many different people alongside the mix of earlier immigrants meant that the U.S., in particular, became known as a "melting pot" of different nationalities and cultures.

Southern European immigrants arriving at Port Melbourne, Australia, in 1948.

AS A MATTER OF FACT

The phrase "melting pot" implies that on arrival in the U.S., immigrants left their own customs, traditions, beliefs, and values behind to form a new culture shared by everyone else. Historians, however, have shown that this was not the case. Different groups had different experiences of adapting to American life. Many immigrants settled alongside people from their home countries and kept their own culture as much as possible. The era of mass immigration led to the building up of ethnic communities in the U.S. that still largely exist today.

Making it for themselves

The 19th- and early 20th-century European immigrants were different from the earlier northern European settlers. Many did not intend to stay in their new countries, but to return home once they had saved up enough money. They often identified with the immigrant dream of making a career for themselves, but they were unlikely to search for a new identity in the way earlier European settlers had done. They kept very much to their own culture and community and, as a result, found it harder to be accepted by earlier immigrant groups.

16

Racial prejudice

The Chinese were one of the first non-European peoples to migrate to Australia and North America in search of work. Because they looked different and had a very different culture, Chinese people were not easily accepted into their new societies.

Newspapers reflected this hostility with stories about their "peculiar" habits. Prejudice, as well as the problems many Chinese had learning English, meant that they relied on their own communities for support and comfort as much as possible.

This postcard from about 1900 depicts New York's Chinese district. Today, "Chinatowns" all over the world are vibrant and bustling places.

SCENE IN CHINATOWN, NEW YORK

LIANG QICHAO'S STORY: THE NEED TO OPEN UP

In the early 20th century, Chinese scholar Liang Qichao (1873–1929) visited communities of his fellow countrymen and women in the U.S. He complained in his writings about the way in which they kept to themselves rather than learning more about their American counterparts.

"Chinese can be clansmen but not citizens. I believe this all the more since my travels in America. There you have those who have left villages and taken on the character of individuals and come and go in the most free of the great cities...and still they cling to the family and clan systems to the exception of other things."

A Mexican-American family in the 1970s. Immigrant communities and families are often very close-knit.

A new generation

The mass movement of people to the U.S., Canada, and Australia could not continue forever. By the early 20th century, governments began to restrict immigrant numbers. Immigrant communities did not grow to the extent they had done previously, but for new arrivals, they provided an important network of support and opportunities.

Many immigrants stayed within the cultural boundaries of their families and close-knit communities. They worked hard and saved money in order to provide their children with an education, so that they, in turn, would be able to move up into professional jobs. Immigrant communities were also known for providing the next generation with inspiration and values that emphasized that they could achieve more if they worked hard.

18

A GREEK-AUSTRALIAN'S STORY: CHANGING ATTITUDES

Hard work was not the only reason why some immigrants kept to themselves. As this Greek-Australian writer shows, prejudice was another major factor:

"In the '70s, the racial conflict was terrible with regards to being a pupil at school or finding a job. Even when working, it was very difficult with racism. Nowadays, life has changed, the country is more multicultural and has accepted the migrants more so than then. As a child and teenager, I found it difficult because I knew I was different than the majority; however, there were enough of us around not to feel too isolated. As I grew older, in my mid to late teens, I began to appreciate this difference and felt proud to come from such a culturally diverse background."

The European experience

In the rush to rebuild Europe after World War II (1939–45), countries such as France and Britain accepted large numbers of immigrants from their former colonies. Indians, Pakistanis, and African-Caribbeans were among the peoples who came to Britain in search of work and new lives, while immigrants from Algeria came to France, fleeing economic hardship and civil war.

New arrivals from the Caribbean disembark from the *Empire Windrush* at Tilbury docks in England, in 1948.

VINCE REID'S STORY: ON THE *WINDRUSH*

Vince Reid was one of the 2,000 Caribbean people who journeyed to Britain on board the ship the *Empire Windrush* in June 1948—the largest arrival of Caribbeans to Britain at the time.

"My parents brought me on the *Windrush*—I had no choice in the matter. They didn't have to—it was obvious they came in search of a better life, better opportunities. It was quite a devastating experience. I was thirteen when I arrived, so I wasn't a man, I was a boy.... I went to school in Kings Cross. I never associated with white people in any significant degree, and then at school I came across real hostility.... To say I had no friends for several years wouldn't be far from the truth."

Our multicultural world

The benefits of multiculturalism

Modern Western societies benefit from multiculturalism in lots of ways. Some benefits are economic—many immigrants have a very strong work ethic and may even take on jobs that other people are not willing to do. Some benefits are cultural, in terms of the creative talents and traditions of different peoples, which often intermingle and emerge as new forms. Most important, perhaps, are the social benefits. Living alongside people from different backgrounds helps broaden horizons and breaks down prejudices.

Old problems

Prejudice still exists, however. Since the early 20th century, most Western countries have experienced waves of negative public opinion and hostility toward ethnic minorities, usually at times when immigration is particularly high. Much of this hostility is directed at newly arrived immigrants, with local populations regarding them as a threat to their jobs and the stability of their culture.

Unlike 50—or even 20—years ago, most of us are used to living alongside people from different backgrounds.

Serving the whole community

The existence of different cultural and ethnic groups in societies has meant that governments now think about how to serve their multiethnic communities better. The police and other public services, for example, work to ensure that everyone can benefit from their services. Public information is translated into many languages so that people with little knowledge of the country's main language know how to vote, access welfare services, report a crime, and get medical care.

Kosovan refugees at an Albanian border checkpoint. The arrival of refugees and immigrants in the West can lead to hostility and racism.

Gaining trust

By trying to cater to their diverse communities, public services in developed countries have also tried to gain more trust with different ethnic groups by employing people from these communities. This increases understanding on both sides and promotes better participation of ethnic minority groups in public life. Problems persist, however. Police forces in developed countries, for example, are often criticized for unfairly picking on people from ethnic minorities.

MALIKA'S STORY: BECOMING ACCEPTED

Malika was born in Morocco and went to Denmark in 1990. She found her first job despite speaking very little Danish. She now works as a bus driver and drives wearing a Muslim headscarf. Often, passengers have stared at her, but Malika learned to deal with it and has found her new job experience very positive.

"I know that many people are a little surprised to see a Muslim woman with a headscarf behind the wheel. That is why I take pains to make some friendly remarks to the passengers. I want to set a good example."

21

Learning about the world

From books to music, the arts express what it is like to live in a multicultural society. They also promote cultural diversity. Today, for example, there are many plays, films, and novels that document the personal stories of immigrants and refugees and how they have coped with leaving their countries and building a new life elsewhere. Cities across the developed world offer a vast selection of cultural events either about other cultures or organized and performed by people from ethnic minority communities.

An Indian singer at the Vancouver Folk Festival in Canada.

Learning about oneself

For many people, being artistically creative can help them cope with the transition of their lives and explore their own cultural identities. This is particularly the case with immigrant communities or people from ethnic minorities. Art can be a way to define how a person feels about him or herself, as well as the means to express hope, anxiety, or frustration with his or her surroundings. For many, taking part in the arts is a useful way to build up confidence.

22

ZERIFE'S STORY: WE ARE!

Zerife and her older sister, alongside other members of Denmark's ethnic minority communities, were invited to take part in a play called *We Are* at a well-known theater in the capital city, Copenhagen. The play told the audience about the actors' lives and dreams in Denmark.

"My family is Kurdish, and we come from Turkey. The story I told in the show was my grandmother's story. She has lived in Denmark for many years but never felt really at home here. The project has definitely changed me as a person, made me more mature and better at working in a group.... What we've been doing there has given me a lot of self-confidence, and it's cool to be in that world where things are so different."

Mutual influence

But art is not just about the individual artist and the messages it gives out to its audience. Different art forms from different cultures continuously influence each other. A Western musician might like certain sounds or elements of music from Africa and incorporate these into his or her own music. On the other hand, artists from different cultures living in the West will be influenced by what they see, hear, and observe in their new surroundings. Artists are often inspired by the very richness and diversity different cultural art forms can bring.

MORIS FARHI'S STORY: THE FORCE OF WRITING

Writer Moris Farhi was born in Turkey in 1935 but has lived and worked in Britain for many years. In an interview, he described his feelings about his identity:

"I've been [in Britain] now 48 years, and I still look upon myself as a Turk. You are really formed in your early youth. Most of the Turkish traditions still remain with me.... I write mainly about persecuted people and persecuted cultures. I believe that pluralism is our greatest wealth, that the more cultures we have, the more languages we speak, the more literatures we produce, the more we can interact with these different cultures, the more humanity will benefit."

World food

Today, more than ever, we enjoy food and goods from around the world and are able to go out to Chinese, Vietnamese, Mexican, Indian, Middle Eastern, and many other different types of restaurants. Ethnic shops and restaurants are vitally important businesses, serving and employing the local community. They also bring part of their culture to a wider audience and introduce people to new tastes and ideas in cooking.

A food stall at a festival offers a mixed ethnic menu.

HANSA'S STORY: A MIXED CULTURAL CUISINE

Hansa's family—originally from Gujarat in India—worked in Uganda until they had to flee the dictatorship there in 1971. Hansa, her parents, and five sisters and brothers ended up in Leeds, England. In 1978, she met her husband, who was from a different Indian caste. They married in secret, against both their parents' wishes. When her two sons were born, Hansa started organizing Indian cooking demonstrations, food stalls, and fundraising events in her community. She eventually opened up a very successful Gujarati vegetarian restaurant in Leeds with the support of her husband.

"[My dishes] draw together my experiences as a Hindu living as a vegetarian in the West. My Indian, East African, and English upbringing all influence the recipes and the choice of ingredients, producing dishes that are a little different and reflect my individual tastes. I hope that they provide an experience that is both physically and mentally satisfying."

Sporting success

But it is not just in the arts or cuisine that people in multicultural societies benefit from the different groups living there. Sports is one area where different people bring different talents and levels of motivation. In the U.S., for example, African-Americans have achieved great success in basketball and boxing, among other sports. Some suggest that black people are better athletes than white people. But experts point out that black athletes train as hard as anyone and often have to overcome social disadvantages to get to the top.

Women basketball players in the U.S.

25

Multicultural schools

Many schools in developed countries, particularly in inner-city areas, educate young people from a wide variety of backgrounds. Schools must consider the different cultural and religious needs of their students and try to ensure that everyone knows something about everyone else's background. Learning about festivals can be a good way to achieve this.

Schools are one of the most important places to experience and learn about multiculturalism.

Extra help

Schools have to think particularly hard about how to help immigrant children integrate into their new school environment. These students may arrive with little knowledge of the language of the host country and may be given additional language classes to help them catch up with the school curriculum. Extra language classes are often also seen as the main tool in helping immigrant children fit into school life.

A TYPICAL STORY: BEING BULLIED

Children of immigrants often face the pressure of parental expectations that they do well at school. If other pupils pick on them, as happened to this young Bengali in Toronto, Canada, they may want to reject their family background completely.

"A bunch of bigger boys were waiting for their target. Since he didn't show up, and since I unknowingly walked by the 'battleground,' I was beaten up. My new jacket [was] ripped in pieces, drenched in saliva.... The following weeks, I was bullied more, for what I thought was because I was brown. So then came my 'white days.' I would detest talking Bangla in public. I could never bring this up at the dinner table, and my other white friends dismissed the whole situation.... I was a total mess."

Teachers try to ensure that all pupils feel included, whatever their backgrounds.

Difficult start

In Europe, some immigrant communities find it particularly hard to be accepted. Many Islamic immigrants from Asia and Africa, for example, often end up unemployed and living in run-down housing areas. The children of these immigrants may also struggle to create opportunities for themselves, especially if there are language problems or they clash with the cultural expectations of their families. But difficult experiences can help young people become stronger.

AÏCHA'S STORY: DOUBLE PERSONALITY

Aïcha's parents emigrated from Algeria to France in the 1950s. Aïcha was born and educated in France. Coming from a family with very traditional values, her parents restricted her movements when she became a teenager. She began to feel trapped and alienated from her parents' culture and no longer felt herself to be a Muslim. In her book *Born In France*, she describes how that felt:

"I continuously saw myself as someone with a double personality. There was the person that was at home—the person my parents wanted me to be—a kind of transitory person. And there was the other person—elsewhere, but that was the one which was really me—the person whose veil I discarded one day."

The fight for equality

In any multicultural society, it is vital that everyone has the same opportunities to access rights and opportunities. The basic principle of equality was set out in the United Nations Universal Declaration of Human Rights—an important international moral code to which most countries have signed up—in 1949. Yet until the 1960s, black people in the U.S. were still unequal to their white counterparts in the eyes of the law. They could not vote, had to send their children to separate schools, and even had to sit away from white people on buses and trains.

STRAND & SEE
NET BLANKES
BEACH & SEA
WHITES ONLY

28 A black man passes a "whites only" sign in South Africa in 1988. Between the 1930s and the 1990s, South Africa created apartheid —one of the severest systems of racial segregation in the world.

JOHN A. POWELL'S STORY: EARLY EXPERIENCES OF RACISM

John is a leading scholar in the U.S. on race and race equality issues. In an interview, he described his experiences growing up in inner-city Detroit as white families moved out to the suburbs when black families moved in.

"I was born in 1947, so I watched Detroit go from a vibrant city to starting to empty out. I watched my mother and father struggling to hold the family together and trying to get housing, and I remember the frustration. And then watching the city starting to die, and literally watching the complexion of the city change. I remember moving to an integrated neighborhood that within a few years became an all-black neighborhood.... I also remember being bused to school, and fighting on the playground because the white kids didn't want us there. I have all these memories. At first they were just experiences, and I didn't quite know how to make sense of them, and didn't necessarily think of them in racial terms, but as I got older and reflected on them, I began to understand."

An ambulance control center. Jobs should be open to anyone, regardless of their ethnic background.

Equality in law

In developed countries, antidiscrimination laws exist to ensure equality and to give people a way to challenge any disadvantages or injustices they may have suffered because of their different ethnic or cultural backgrounds. These laws mean that, in theory, no one is allowed to be discriminated against, harassed, or in any way abused because of their skin color, religion, or place of birth.

Discrimination in practice

The existence of such laws does not, of course, stop discrimination from happening. American research, for example, shows that black and Hispanic people in the U.S. are still far more likely to be targeted by the police than white Americans. This means they are more likely to be arrested, too. Yet statistics show that there is no more likelihood of black and Hispanic people committing crimes than their white counterparts.

SILVIA'S STORY: GETTING JUSTICE

Silvia is Latin American and worked illegally as a secretary for an insurance company in San Francisco. When her employer failed to pay her wages and working conditions became intolerable, Silvia filed a legal claim for the money she was owed. To retaliate, her employer informed the U.S. immigration authorities that Silvia had worked illegally. But a court in California found that she was entitled to her wages. It also said that it was not acceptable for employers to retaliate in this way.

Equality and work

Finding work and improving career opportunities is an important area in which equality laws can have a direct impact on the lives of members of ethnic minorities and immigrant communities. Research shows that immigrants, for example, are far less likely to find work than the local population. This makes it difficult for them to access further education, move out from the impoverished areas they often live in, and improve their standard of life.

DENG'S STORY: WANTING TO WORK

When Deng returned to his home country, Sudan, after studying at Cairo University, he had to flee to avoid being forcefully recruited into the Sudanese army. He came to Britain and applied for asylum. Even though he was allowed to work, finding a job was impossible.

"When I arrived in [Britain] in 1994, I was very [eager] to put my skills and qualifications to good use. As well as my studies in Egypt, I had a Master's degree in second language curriculum development and more than ten years' experience of teaching and translation work in both Egypt and Sudan. However, I found it almost impossible to find a job here, even though the Home Office had given me permission to work. Although I wrote over 100 job applications, I only got one interview, and even then I was unsuccessful."

Today, Deng has permission to remain in Britain. He works for a charity to help other refugees in similar situations.

Positive action

In many developed countries, it is illegal for an employer to give a job to a white person if there is a person from an ethnic minority who is more qualified to do the job. It is also illegal for employers to treat people unfairly because of who they are. Some companies have policies that actively encourage people from ethnic minorities to apply for jobs.

Negative perceptions

Fears about immigration can make it harder for first, second, and third generation immigrants to enter the job market. Negative reporting in the media often fuels people's perception that the arrival of immigrants is not good for society. It can lead to assumptions that immigrants lack qualifications or talent and are only in the country to live off benefits. In direct contrast, many governments are now openly acknowledging that immigrant communities contribute hugely to the economy.

AS A MATTER OF FACT

Governments in some developed countries recognize that immigrants make important contributions to their economies. Most immigrants are of working age and are highly motivated to work, and therefore pay taxes. Immigrants' financial contributions are difficult to work out, but the British government has estimated that immigrants pay $4.5 billion more in taxes than they get in benefits.

In Western countries, many senior-level jobs are still dominated by white people. Equality works in theory, but often not in practice.

Understanding differences

Children performing a dance to mark the Hindu festival of Holi.

Multicultural societies are marked by their religious diversity. Many developed countries are no longer home to one dominant religion, such as Christianity, but a variety of faiths, including Islam, Judaism, Hinduism, Buddhism, and Sikhism. The benefits of a "multifaith" society include the possibility of people with different religions being enriched by each other's beliefs and traditions and working together on international issues such as helping the victims of the Asian tsunami in 2004 or dealing with poverty in Africa.

DYAB ABOU JAHJAH'S STORY: PUTTING THE RECORD STRAIGHT

Dyab Abou Jahjah is 31. He was born in Lebanon and now lives in Belgium. He was accused of inciting street riots in Antwerp after a mentally ill Belgian man murdered a Muslim Moroccan schoolteacher. Abou Jahjah is very critical of European governments' attitude toward their Islamic communities:

"America's race laws are more advanced than here. I have relatives in Detroit, and they are Arab Americans but they feel American. I don't feel European. Europe needs to make its concept of citizenship inclusive to all cultures and religions. I'm a practicing Muslim, but I'm not a freak. I'm not a fundamentalist."

Religious tensions

Different religions, however, can cause considerable tension within communities. Ever since the terrorist attacks in the U.S. on September 11, 2001, some people in Western countries have viewed Islam with suspicion. One charge leveled at Muslims is that they are religious fanatics who support violent activities to promote their faith. In fact, like any religion, fanatics are only a tiny minority among Muslim people.

Different practices

Different religious practices have also caused debate and even court actions. Muslim girls and women in Britain and France, for example, have had to fight for their right to wear the hijab, the traditional Muslim headscarf. The charge of religious persecution is one that Western governments must take very seriously—their laws and constitutions commit them to ensuring all religions are allowed freedom of expression.

JOANNE'S STORY: NEW VALUES

Joanne was brought up as a French-speaking Catholic in Canada in the 1950s. She tells how new values began to replace old ones.

"Neighborhoods became ethnically diverse, and children began to speak English outside the home.... [Then] the turbulent '60s changed a lot of traditions, customs, and a way of life. Our church began celebrating mass in both languages. More mixed marriages were occurring within the family, and the churches seem to acquire a more tolerant attitude."

Turkish women in Berlin, Germany, wearing Muslim headscarves. Some people argue that the scarves should not be worn in nonreligious schools.

33

Arranged marriages

As immigration from non-European countries has increased in developed countries, ethnic groups from certain African and Asian countries have brought with them cultural practices that clash with Western values. It is, for example, common for African and Asian families to arrange the marriages of their children. This practice can cause difficulties for young people, who are faced with balancing the wishes of their parents against the liberal ideas of Western society.

An Indian couple on their wedding day.

PAVI'S STORY: MY MOTHER'S ARGUMENT

Pavi, who is from a Hindu family, was opposed to having an arranged marriage. Here she discusses her mother's reasons why such a marriage was a good idea:

"My parents always felt it was so much better to first be married, and within that covenant context, learn to love each other. I didn't want to have an arranged marriage, and we had all kinds of debate on the matter. My mother's argument was that she had given birth to me, raised me, knew me inside and out, even though I thought I was all grown up and mature, and loved me like nobody else ever could—plus she understood women better than I did, and knew the realities of marriage from the inside. So who better to find me someone who would be a perfect fit?"

34

Honor killings

For immigrant women from different cultures, adapting to life in the West can be particularly difficult. They are often expected to conform to traditional roles and values in the family, may have very little contact with the outside world, and may not learn the language of their home country. There have been cases in developed countries in which husbands and brothers have even killed a female family member for refusing to conform to traditional values and bringing shame onto the family.

FADIME'S STORY: A FAMILY TRAGEDY

Fadime Sahindal immigrated to Sweden with her Turkish Kurdish family in the 1980s. She was 26 when her father shot her dead because she refused an arranged marriage and had a relationship with a Swedish man. Before her death in 2002, Fadime appealed for help and even spoke in the Swedish parliament about her situation:

"My parents' view was that family and relatives were the center of things, and I therefore had to think about what was best for the family before thinking about my own well-being.... But in contrast to my parents, I lived in and was part of Swedish society. I went to Swedish school every day, I ate Swedish food, I had Swedish friends and watched Swedish television. I therefore began to stretch the boundaries more and more...[and] continued to meet my Swedish friends."

Fitting in

Many different cultural practices are, however, easily absorbed into the fabric of multicultural societies. Some practices move beyond ethnic communities into the mainstream. Examples include the African and Caribbean traditions of carnival, the origins of which lie in West African celebrations and festivals held by slaves, and the Asian practices of vegetarianism, meditation, yoga, and martial arts.

The Notting Hill Carnival, shown here, has had a big impact on British culture. Up to a million people attend the carnival in West London each year.

A question of identity

Many people, at some point in life, will question what their identity is. For different people, it can mean very different things. For immigrants, the question of identity can be a difficult one. Many will continue to feel a loyalty to their own country despite living in another country for many years. Their readiness to integrate into their new surroundings can also depend on why they left. Many refugees struggle to come to terms with the changes they have gone through.

A mother and son prepare food for the Muslim festival of Eid al-Adha ("feast of the sacrifice").

VAIRA VIKE-FREIBERGA'S STORY: FEELING LOST

Vaira Vike-Freiberga's family fled from Latvia to Canada when the Soviet Union invaded Latvia during World War II. In 1997, Vaira, a psychology professor, returned to Latvia and two years later was elected as its president. In a speech to mark the 50th anniversary of the Refugee Convention—the international law that protects refugees worldwide—she described the identity crisis many refugees experience:

"You are living outside of space and of time, you have no roots, you have no past, you don't know whether you have a future, you have no rights, you have no papers, sometimes you haven't even got your name, and you have to pinch yourself to reassure yourself that yes, I am alive, I am me, I am a human being, I am a person. Do I count in this world? I don't know, I'll wait until tomorrow."

Between two cultures

Young people in immigrant communities usually find it easier than their parents to adapt to a Western lifestyle and identify with their new country. They mix with locals at school and tend to have a better knowledge of the country's language and a desire to do well in the future. For some, this can lead to a desire to reject their family's culture. Others rediscover their own cultural heritage as they grow older.

Vietnamese-American teenagers in California. Children of immigrants are often good at mixing their families' customs with mainstream culture.

JENNIFER'S STORY: A DEEP CONNECTION

Jennifer is in her early 30s and emigrated from South Korea to the U.S. when she was 6. She went back to Korea to study and learn more about the country of her birth.

"There are many Koreans all around the world who miss their homeland. This is wonderful. However, I was very deeply disappointed by the fact that Koreans are not at all interested in these visiting students. While I was studying Korean history in graduate school in Korea, I was so surprised by the number of countries from which second generation Koreans came. Even though Koreans are scattered across the entire world, they still have a deep sense of home. What a joy that there are so many second and third generation Koreans who feel so deeply about Korea!"

Motivation

The ability to integrate today, as in the past, depends on motivation. Researchers have found that while local people have become very aware of their rights and may demand better pay and working conditions, immigrants are often different. They are less concerned about their rights in terms of benefits and work obligations, and more concerned about having a job—even if the pay is low— to get a foothold in the job market and to get ahead. Often they succeed, and this makes them identify strongly with their new country.

37

The importance of citizenship

For immigrants wanting to be a part of the societies in which they now live, becoming a citizen is an important process. Citizenship gives immigrants the rights to vote, to stand for elections, and to be protected by their government when they travel abroad. Western countries have introduced citizenship tests for immigrants who want to become nationals. These test language skills and knowledge of the history and culture of the country. Many immigrants feel proud to be able to take the test and become a citizen in this way.

New U.S. citizens taking the oath of loyalty on Ellis Island, New York.

JETTE'S STORY: TAKING THE AMERICAN OATH

Many countries also require their new citizens to take an oath of loyalty. Jette, who left Denmark in 1988 to join her husband in the U.S., did just that.

"February 1, 1997, turned out to be the day that I finally took the oath. We set out on a crisp Saturday morning with 346 other people bearing exotic names from all over the world. We came in all shades of pink and brown, but the unifying characteristics were our bated breaths, shivering hands, and pounding hearts, realizing this was it. We could still have changed our minds and run out as fast as we could, but everyone seemed determined, encouraged by the many smiling friends and family members who had come to share this important moment in our lives.... Do I feel differently now? Not really. I still count and do math in Danish, I still have to spell my name, and I still have to account for my accent now and again. What *is* different is that when [the] President gets up and starts a speech with the words 'My fellow Americans,' I feel I belong here."

New identities

For many people, identity is less about the decision to integrate into the mainstream or remain true to their parents' and grandparents' culture. It is more about shaping new identities that reflect both their family backgrounds and the place they live in today. These identities are reflected in descriptions such as "Greek-Australian," "Mexican-American," and "Black British." There are many songs, films, and books that express what it is to have a mixed identity, informed by one's past, present, and hopes for the future.

A diverse crowd watching a concert in the Barbes-Rochechouart district of Paris, France, which is home to many North African immigrants.

SHANE'S STORY: MIXED ORIGINS

Shane's father is a white American, and his mother's parents are of black and Native American origin, respectively. He is proud of his racial heritage, but can get frustrated by people's attitudes:

"People think I'm Greek, Italian, Puerto Rican, every damn thing under the sun, Panamanian, Argentinean, Serbian, Jewish. In New York, more cosmopolitan people realize there are shades of gray. And where I'm from, you're black, you're white, or you're Indian. That's it. You're one or the other.... Why is it that I have to explain things to whites and blacks? Why can't I look at you as an individual and your characteristics as something more than your race? Race is a problem because people make it a problem. Just get on with it—get over it."

The multicultural future

A continuing dilemma

Societies in developed countries continue to face a dilemma. On the one hand, they accept cultural diversity and the advantages that multiculturalism can bring. On the other hand, they are concerned about levels of immigration and the tensions this can create between different groups. Some people argue that it is up to each of us to accept how other people want to live. "Other people" want the same thing as everyone else—to fit in.

CAMILLA'S STORY: WHERE DO I FIT IN?

Camilla is a writer living in the U.S. She was born in South Korea but was adopted and educated in Norway. Here she describes her thoughts on adapting to different cultures.

"When people ask me: 'Where are you from?' I've answered: 'I'm from Norway, but I was born in South Korea.' And sometimes to avoid further questions, I've also answered, 'I'm from South Korea.' This is a very typical reaction among Korean adoptees in Norway or other European countries.

"I grew up with four other siblings, one Norwegian brother and two sisters, and one other Korean adopted sister.

"Being adopted means to relate to being different in many ways. I think what I really want to say is that being different in terms of not being 'normal' or looking normal (meaning Norwegian, blonde, Scandinavian) is also a question of relating to what is different around you. You have to accept that others think you are from China, because you are from a different place. And if it's not China, what place is it? And how do I feel about it?

"By acknowledging this, I'm showing that it is possible to explore this unknown place that you have inside you, a place you might have forgotten until now. But whatever answers you might find about your cultural inheritance, your memories, and so on, they will always generate new questions, new territories to explore. It's all a matter of getting a grasp of life itself."

Italian policemen question new arrivals. Fears about immigration can stop people from seeing the good things different cultures bring to societies.

Integration or preservation

Some politicians maintain that ethnic minority communities should do more to integrate into Western societies. Such thinking has led many European countries, including Britain, the Netherlands, and Denmark, to consider ways of encouraging integration. The Netherlands, for example, is looking into setting up special tests for non-Western immigrants to see whether they are making efforts to integrate. Immigrants would have to show that they are competent in the Dutch language and also understand the cultural norms of Dutch society.

A changing world

Multiculturalism, however, makes it harder to pin down

Neighbors chatting on a street corner. It is up to each of us to accept and learn from other people.

the cultural norms of a particular country that everyone should accept. This trend is set only to increase. Governments acknowledge the economic importance of immigrants, so it is unlikely immigration will stop. And, whatever our backgrounds, we have all become citizens in a multicultural world thanks to the Internet, digital television, and global travel—as well as the experience of living with people whose backgrounds may be very different from our own.

Glossary

asylum Special legal immigration status given to people who are recognized as refugees according to the 1951 Convention on Refugees.

asylum seeker A person seeking asylum in another country because he or she fears persecution or danger in his or her own country.

Australasia The islands of the Southern Pacific Ocean, including Australia, New Zealand, and New Guinea.

British Empire The territories controlled by Britain from the 17th to mid-20th centuries as it expanded trade and conquered new lands. At its height, the British Empire covered almost 40 percent of the world's land.

citizenship If a person has a country's citizenship, it means he or she is a national of that country and holds that country's passport.

colonization The process of establishing a new settlement or colony, usually overseas from a home country.

colony Usually refers to an area of land controlled by a state that is overseas or abroad from it.

developed countries High-income countries where people have a high standard of living. These are usually found in Europe and North America, but also include Australia, New Zealand, and Japan.

developing countries Low- and middle-income countries where people have a lower standard of living and not as many goods and services available to them as in developed countries.

discrimination Treating people differently, and usually unfairly, because of their age, sex, nationality, color, or because of a disability.

economic growth When the production of goods and services increases, more profit is being made and more jobs are created.

emigrant A person leaving his or her home country to live permanently in another country.

European Union The union of 25 European countries, which works toward shared economic and social goals.

exploitation In a workplace situation, treating employees in a way that suits the interests of the business without respecting the interests of the individual.

fanatic People are fanatic if they are too enthusiastic or even obsessive about what they believe in or support, such as a religion, a pop star, or a football team.

freeman A person who enjoys all the privileges of being a free citizen.

fundamentalist A person who supports a religion or a political party with such extreme enthusiasm that he or she does not like others to criticize the cause.

human rights Set of rights that everyone in the world should be entitled to, such as the right to free speech, the right to basic education, and the right to move freely to other countries.

immigrant A person who has moved permanently to another country to live and work.

immigration laws Laws that set out the circumstances under which people can live and work in a country not their own.

integrate To adapt to the values and customs of the society in which one lives.

liberal A person is liberal when he or she is open-minded and tolerant of other people's opinions and supports the idea of individual freedom and democracy.

migrant A person going to work in another country, usually for a limited time only.

missionary A person who is sent by a church to another area or country to promote its religion. Modern-day missionaries often carry out humanitarian work, such as helping the poor.

persecution Being punished, tortured, or mistreated by a government or a military group, usually because of one's political or religious beliefs or ethnic backround.

racism Judging people or behaving unfairly to them because of their skin color or ethnic background.

refugees People living abroad who are recognized under international law as being unable to return to their home country for fear of their lives or freedom.

refugee camp A settlement, usually temporary, that develops when people flee their homes during times of war or famine to go to a safer area near the borders of their own country.

rights Claims to freedom, equal treatment, and resources that are guaranteed by law.

visa Official permission from a foreign country to visit it. This is usually given by the country's embassy, which puts a stamp in a person's passport to show that a visa has been granted.

work ethic Believing in the personal benefits and advantages of carrying out work diligently and thoroughly.

World War II The biggest world conflict in history, involving most of the world's countries, fought from 1939 until 1945.

Web connections

International Organizations

International Organization for Migration (IOM)
www.iom.int

International Labor Organization (ILO)
www.ilo.org

United Nations (UN)
www.un.org

United Nations High Commissioner for Refugees (UNHCR)
www.unhcr.ch

Nongovernmental organizations

Anti-Slavery International
www.antislavery.org
Oldest human rights organization, set up in 1839 to campaign against slavery and forced labor.

Australian Refugee Council
www.refugeecouncil.org.au
Covers information about asylum and refugees in Australia.

British Refugee Council
www.refugeecouncil.org.uk
Leading refugee charity in Britain, helping newly arrived asylum seekers and recognized refugees.

Civil Rights
www.civilrights.org
A U.S.-based organization that provides an on-line forum to work against discrimination in all its forms and to build up public understanding toward social and economic justice.

Independent Race and Refugee Network
www.irr.org.uk
An independent educational charity carrying out research on race relations issues worldwide.

Minority Rights Group
www.minorityrights.org
A human rights organization that works for the rights of minorities worldwide and promotes cooperation between communities.

Survival International
www.survival-international.org
An organization that helps tribal people defend their lives, protect their lands, and determine their own futures.

Index